Manifestation Angels

Divine Messages to Manifest Your Desires with Joy and Ease

Heart-Based Manifesting, Book 2

Copyright Elena G. Rivers © 2022

All rights reserved. No part of this publication may be reproduced, stored in a retrieval system, or transmitted, in any form or by any means, electronic, mechanical, photocopying, recording, or otherwise, without the author and the publishers' prior written permission.

The scanning, uploading, and distributing this book via the Internet or any other means without the author's permission are illegal and punishable by law. Please purchase only authorized electronic editions and do not participate in or encourage electronic piracy of copyrighted materials.

Elena G. Rivers © Copyright 2022 - All rights reserved.

ISBN: 978-1-80095-078-8

Legal Notice:

This book is copyright protected—it for personal use only.

Disclaimer Notice:

Please note that the information contained in this book is for inspirational and entertainment purposes only. Every attempt has been made to provide accurate, up-to-date, and completely reliable information. No warranties of any kind are expressed or implied. Readers acknowledge that the author is not engaging in the rendering of legal, financial, health, medical, or professional advice. By reading this book, the reader agrees that under no circumstances are we responsible for any losses, direct or indirect, which are incurred due to the use of the information contained within this book, including, but not limited to, errors, omissions, or inaccuracies. The information provided in this book is for entertainment purposes only. If you are struggling with serious problems, including chronic illness, mental instability, or legal issues, please consult with your local registered health care or legal professional as soon as possible. This book is not a substitute for professional or legal advice.

Contents

Message #1 To Believe...But How? What Does It Really Mean to Believe? 6

Message #2 Embody to Manifest – The Art of Becoming What You Want 13

Message #3 Attracting Unlimited Abundance (No More Money Fears!) 24

Message #4 Don't Help Others without Protecting Your Energy (Important Message for Empaths) ... 36

Message #5 Your Desires Are Divine – Time to Release Fear, Guilt, and Shame! 51

Message #6 The Science of Taking Aligned Action 60

Message #7 Freedom from Negative Thoughts 72

Message #8 The Law of You- It's Time to Create Your Own Manifesting Rules! (Because You Can!) 81

Conclusion – Trust Yourself 88

Join Our Manifestation Newsletter and Get a Free eBook 90

More Books & Workbooks by Elena G. Rivers 92

Message #1 To Believe...But How? What Does It Really Mean to Believe?

You probably already know that believing in what you want is the key to manifesting your desires. But, what does it really mean "to believe"? We know that many heart-centered people have amazing desires and really want to believe in them but don't know how. They lose their faith and revert back to where they were before. We don't want that to happen to you!

At the same time, we know that by guiding you on how to believe by sharing our divine messages through Elena, you have the power to change your life and the lives of others. Together we can raise the vibration of the planet.

And you can help us do so, just by being you. Even if you're not a healer or a teacher, you will soon find out how to turn your life into a truly magical experience while helping others do the same, just by being you and achieving your desires.

So, first things first. You need to learn how to believe in what you desire. Have you ever actually thought about believing and what it really means? Seriously, take a moment and think about it. Stop reading for a few minutes. And take note of this Universal truth- *if you really believe in what you want, you will attract what you want.* This has been written so many times in so many different spiritual books.

But most people on Earth don't know how to believe. If that's you, don't worry, it's not your fault. And it's not your teachers' fault either. It's just that over the years and centuries, the true angelic message of faith and believing got distorted. People in power didn't want you to know this. They wanted you to stay disempowered.

But there's a way out! Reading and applying this chapter alone, even if you skip the rest of this book (but we have the feeling you will carry on reading), has the power to offer you a quantum leap and become a manifesting magnet.

If you've been around any LOA, manifesting, or spiritual community...

Or even general self-help, or entrepreneur self-help community...

You've probably heard about the importance of believing.

Believe in yourself.

Believe in your desire.

Believe in your vision.

Believe in your passion.

Believe in your goals.

Etc etc.

But what does it even mean?

Is it only about saying that you believe?

Or about declaring how much you believe?

Mindlessly reciting some affirmations trying to convince yourself that you believe?

Or perhaps trying to prove to others how much you believe in your goals?

In reality, *believing* means fusing yourself with your desires and being your desires...

Well, this will make everything so much easier!

Let's take a look at the word BELIEVE.

It's created out of two words:

BE + LIVE.

So, if you really believe in something, you ARE and LIVE it.

In other words, you EMBODY it.

So, when you think about your desire, whatever it is, do you really BELIEVE in it by being and living it? Can you embody it?

From Elena's personal experience, one of her biggest manifestation blocks was subconsciously fighting her desires.

She wanted one thing (such as financial stability and love) on the outside.

And she kept mindlessly saying, "Oh yea, I believe I could reach financial freedom...."

But, on the inside, she was fighting her desires instead of embodying them.

She wanted money but was scared of financial success.

She wanted love but was scared of loving and being loved.

But when she fully understood what it meant to BELIEVE, she finally analyzed her old manifesting efforts by tuning into her inner wisdom and staying open to receiving our messages. She got rid of what was blocking her.

She released all her doubts and fears. She understood that these were only the fallacies of her own mind because her mind lacked the true belief in her desires.

She began taking action from a place of total confidence and unlimited empowerment. She decided to share her message with others simply by embodying her beliefs.

Remember that you can choose to start embodying your desires whenever and however you want. It's never too late to change your life!

Your power is always in the present moment.

You can choose to create various affirmations with the word: "Embody" (and just play around with words that feel good to you).

But you can also visualize, do mirror work, or script about your desires, all from a place of already having them.

Simply be mindful of your feelings and state of being! Take an honest look at your manifesting journey, all from a place of love and authenticity. Don't beat yourself up. Ask yourself if you genuinely believe in what you desire? Tune into your inner wisdom and ask yourself: "How can I live and be my desire?"

Meditate on that question. Whenever you're ready, proceed to the following message, where we will dive deeper into the concept of embodiment, specifically, how to embody to manifest.

Message #2 Embody to Manifest – The Art of Becoming What You Want

Embodiment is one of the most critical pieces of the manifesting puzzle. And everyone will experience it differently, in their own unique way!

First of all, let's look at the word: *Embodiment*.

It consists of different words such as:

I am, body, movement...

So, what do you embody when you take an honest look at your current state of being?

What do you really embody? Who are you? What kind of energy are you moving with the current of your thoughts?

Now, of course, we're not talking about some "dress for success" thing, although there's nothing wrong with that, and you can choose to dress for success in whatever way feels good to you.

We're talking about your inner state. Your energy. Because it's your internal state and energy that manifest.

For example, before getting in touch with us and staying open to receiving our divine guidance, Elena was desperately trying to embody money, love, and success.

But that embodiment wasn't really inside her. It wasn't in her body.

Her body was full of fear, lack, hatred, and resentment.

She would spend most of her days in worry and complaining. Then, she somehow tried to fight and manipulate the outside world or the sad reality she created with her unhappy inner states.

Even when she first discovered LOA, she didn't have any consistent success with it.

Because she wasn't genuinely embodying any of these beautiful teachings (that her New Self always feels so inspired to share with others).

We are sharing our messages through Elena because we know her story will resonate with many people who felt disappointed after trying to manifest their desires. As we already told you in the introduction, our message is to make people happy, healthy, loved, and abundant. We want to raise the collective vibration, and just by reading this book and applying some of the concepts we share, you are helping us tremendously.

So, back to Elena (before she became the new Elena by choosing to follow our guidance).

Yes, she could manifest some success here and there.

She could make some money here and there by applying hard work and very forced mental effort. Or some hot business opportunities that were never sustainable enough.

But she would always get back to her default state in the end. Her manifestations and achievements were never steady or secure because she didn't feel stable or secure.

Her inner state, embodiment, body, mind, and soul were filled with negativity, lack, worry, and fear.

Then, she would apply lots of effort to "try and be positive." She tried very hard to reach elevated states of motivation, inspiration, and happiness. And yes, she could often experience them, for example, when attending workshops or seminars.

And she could manifest something, only to lose it later.

Finally, she said: "OK, enough. I am done!"

She had an intuitive look at the word *embodiment*.

She asked herself: "What do I really embody?"

She knew something was blocking her. She knew she could be more. And she prayed for answers.

She meditated for answers. And we sent her the answers she needed. We knew she was willing to receive our guidance and act on it. Just like you are right now!

Then, it hit her...

She had to get rid of what was blocking her first. She had to get rid of what she was, what was in her body, and the energies she was moving with her thoughts, actions, and feelings...

I am + Body + Movement = EMBODY

So, she began a little manifestation reset, and she stopped practicing LOA techniques.

Of course, her intention wasn't to stop practicing them forever.

She knew she'd come back to them. She enjoyed them.

And she also knew she had to make peace with herself from within herself. She had to get rid of her old embodiments, such as constant fear, lack, and worry.

She began what she likes to call neutralization, a stabilization period...

A little inner detox she so desperately needed.

Now, there are different healing modalities you can experiment with, such as Reiki, energy healing, NLP,

Faster EFT, EFT tapping, all kinds of meditations, yoga...

It's really up to you.

Elena's process is as follows:

She scans her body inside out. She asks herself: *is my state neutral? Or is it too negative or too obsessively positive from the energy "of trying to be positive to manifest"?*

Then, she says to herself- *I release and let it go. I welcome peace and neutrality.*

Then, she does something to move her body (to release what's in her body and what she embodies if it's not aligned with what she desires).

She goes for a walk, does yoga, dances, or practices EFT tapping. Sometimes she may do a different healing modality, such as Reiki. But, this message isn't really about modalities and which one is the best.

Because the one you choose and honestly believe in (believe= be + live, so it means that you practice it regularly) will work for you.

This message is about opening your eyes to what may be blocking your manifestations. You can get rid of your blocks and reach a neutral, peaceful state that opens a whole new gate of possibilities.

For example, the old version of Elena would never write and share such a personal message, and she would feel too ashamed to channel messages from angelic entities.

Her old self would be too scared of rejection or judgment.

"What if people think I've gone mad...?"

So, her old self wouldn't even embody any right choices for her. She kept on missing so many opportunities for beautiful synchronistic and effortless manifestations. Yet, she would keep affirming she was confident and authentic. Can you see this massive lack of alignment here?

In other words, before transforming herself and embodying her desires, Elena could reach some positive, sometimes highly positive states when doing

LOA techniques, but her predominant inner state lacked alignment and was full of blocks.

So, she was standing in her own way.

But, ever since she has integrated our teachings and the knowledge of embodiment into her life, she can catch and transform any misalignments almost instantly.

By choosing to embody what you want, you attract what you want. How to embody health and vibrant energy? Tune into your inner guidance. Ask your deep inner self: "How can I embody more health and energy?"

Stay in a meditative state for as long as you need to find your answers. As you do so, keep releasing any doubts or fears. Allow yourself to be healthy. Then, choose to embody health by being and living a truly healthy lifestyle.

As they say, different strokes for different folks. Instead of following the crowd or the latest diet or supplement trend, you will need to figure out what works best for you. Start by diving into your divine essence to access your answers.

Visualize yourself being healthy and energized. Keep affirming that your body gets younger and younger every day. Feel it. Live it as your new truth. Ask for guidance and inspiration, and don't be afraid to try new things. If you get a sudden download to try a yoga class, go for it!

Don't create any stories or excuses around it. Stop focusing on what you did wrong in the past. Many people struggle with losing weight, or eating a healthy, nutritious diet, because they keep rehearsing some old stories of how they failed or got off track.

If you ever catch yourself thinking such negative thoughts or telling negative stories, immediately say: *cancel-cancel, that's not who I am.* And focus your mind and heart on visualizing your desired outcome.

The same mindset and heartset apply to anything you want, such as money, career, or relationships.

Take a few deep breaths. Focus your attention on your heart. Tune in. Ask for guidance. We are always willing to help you!

Simply ask: *"I desire to manifest more money into my life. I am open to receiving new income streams. Please send me inspiration and guidance. I am willing to do my part"*.

Ask, embody, be patient, be grateful, and receive!

When you choose to embody something, go all in! Embody the energy of money and abundance by being grateful for all the money coming to you and the bills you pay. See abundance everywhere.

(You will learn more about attracting abundance in the chapter on abundance. As for now, we are slowly building up your positivity and manifesting muscle and raising your vibration.)

The most fundamental lesson on embodying money and abundance is to stop complaining about the lack of money and release any resentment towards people who have or don't have money. Release any need to judge, and instead, use your creative energies to fully channel what you want.

You can also embody a new relationship by choosing to be it. For example, if you want other people to listen to you and feel understood, give the same value to others. Elena had lots of blocks around sharing her writing with the world because she felt scared of rejection (due to some past events in her childhood). She kept repeating the same old childhood and teen story about how she felt misunderstood or ignored. But after getting in touch with us and receiving guidance, she learned how to embody what she wanted.

She asked herself: *"How can I make other people feel understood and cared for? How can I soothe their inner states? How can I lead with empathy?"*

She also did some inner child work and decided to take care of the little Elena inside her.

From there, things really took off for her. And now it's your turn. Your quantum leap is just around the corner!

Ask yourself how you want to be treated by other people. And treat others exactly the way you want to be treated. Have your values and stick to them. Embody them to attract them. It's as simple as that. Embodiment speaks louder than words.

Message #3 Attracting Unlimited Abundance (No More Money Fears!)

Most people decide to study the Law of Attraction because they desire to live more abundant lives. For some, it may be a better-paying job. For others, it may be more streams of income. Some may desire a fulfilling career that allows them to be well compensated for their work. For some, it may be manifesting more clients, or an online business they can run from anywhere in the world.

At the same time, some may desire to win the lottery or manifest some unexpected money. And some may want to manifest more travels and unforgettable moments with their loved ones.

Different strokes for different folks, as they say!

But what if we told you that none of the above examples is really abundance? Yes, they can reflect abundance. And everyone deserves to have their dreams and desires that give them hope and motivation.

But true abundance is beyond words…

And true abundance is a state that happens well beyond what your mind can comprehend…

It's something you need to experience for yourself by becoming a diligent student of your own awareness and inner states.

Also, remember that you are your best teacher and mentor. Yes, it's definitely helpful to get guidance from someone who has walked the path (and is still on it). But, at the same time, you need to be independent in your ways of thinking, feeling, acting, and investigating your inner states.

For example, during the early stages of wanting to manifest money and abundance, many people seek out mentors who can help them. This is what Elena decided to do, and it made perfect sense to her. Or it made sense to her logical mind. Because, like so many people on this journey, she ignored her heart. She was very driven by a desperate desire to manifest more money out of lack and fear.

Now she's not ashamed to admit that because she understands that her story and example alone can help many people on their manifesting journeys.

So, what happened is that Elena, using her logic alone, hired a mentor. Someone who was very successful and taught both mindset and business strategy.

And that individual was very smart and experienced and offered a lot of great advice that benefited many people.

So why did Elena not succeed in using his programs? Simple...it was her inner state. Her internal state of negative feelings. Past failures and desperation only amplified the state of lack inside her.

Not only that...

As she got caught up in chasing and chasing, she disconnected from her heart. And her heart was screaming: *No, wait, this person is not meant to* mentor you. *His work is excellent, but he's meant to work with people with different values.*

For example, one of the things the above-mentioned mentor recommended was going to five-star resorts and immersing oneself in luxury. That is how he taught his students to align themselves with abundance. "Go to that expensive hotel and stay there for several nights. Imagine all this luxury is yours. Imagine it's your everyday life.".

And, there's nothing wrong with that. It worked for many people…

But, once again, Elena's inner state was screaming…

Come on, you are here only for a week. And then you are back to the same old, same old. Hmmm, should you really be spending all your money on that hotel? Is it really worth it?

As you can see, her inner state was far from abundant.

At the same time, Elena's old mentor recommended something that many people in the coaching industry recommend. If you want to attract high-paying clients, you also need to invest in high-level mentorship.

And once again, there's nothing wrong with that if it feels good to you, makes you feel abundant, and is entirely congruent with how you want to run your business or live your life.

But, it's all about checking your inner state first. It's your internal state of abundance that manifests.

You could be surrounded by expensive items and luxury (that you either own or rent) but still feel unworthy and undeserving on the inside, therefore amplifying the feelings of lack. Believe it or not, some rich people still feel very poor on the inside. And even if they keep manifesting more money through hard and smart work and business systems or investments, their inner states are drained, and they don't feel happy.

At the same time, you could make a simple sandwich and eat it in your local park and feel immense feelings of abundance.

Do what feels right for you and your heart.

For years, Elena feared accepting discounts because she had a limiting belief that it would make her a cheapskate.

This is what she was taught by many of her early business mentors. And once again; different strokes for different folks!

There's no judgment here. Some people like expensive things. And only expensive things.

The number one lesson from this chapter is to scan your awareness. Study your awareness. Embrace your feelings and ask yourself (using your heart, not your mind): "Is this method or strategy really right for me? Who am I? How do I feel?".

Who are you? Well, you are what you hold within you. And you manifest who you are...

So, when you look at it that way, manifesting is very easy; *it's your predominant inner state that manifests.*

Of course, we don't want to make you feel bad or scared by the above statement. At the end of the day, every human, even the most positive one, experiences negative thoughts and states from time to time. Why? Because they are alive. And human. So don't feel bad about having negative thoughts. All you need to do is make a choice. You can shift to positive and empowering thoughts whenever you want. Simply think about the things you love!

Now, let's get back to your abundance awareness...

You can embrace the feelings of abundance wherever and whenever you want. For example, going to your local supermarket and finding excellent deals and discounts could make you feel abundant. How does it feel? Can you embrace and amplify the feelings of gratitude?

You can shift your inner states whenever you want. All it takes is mastering your awareness and using it as your GPS.

A person could receive amazing deals and discounts but complain that they didn't win something huge or didn't manifest a significant pay rise.

Remember that you always have a choice. Those little daily situations allow us to choose between inner states and focus on gratitude and positivity. Do this as much as you can, and you will be very abundant and thriving. You will be a magnet to many fantastic opportunities and situations that you were unaware of before.

All you need to do is tune in your inner state of abundance as you go about your day.

You can embrace this mindset, or better said, heartset, as you go shopping and pay your bills. How do you feel when you pay for something? Most people feel some kind of negative emotion.

But, at the same time, they have a choice. They can choose to tune in their inner states of abundance and express their gratitude for the product or service they purchased. They can even bless the service provider!

These ideas may seem weird to most people who may not be quite familiar with manifesting lifestyle. They may think: *"But aren't we supposed to feel good when we receive money and complain when we have to give it to someone to pay for something?"*.

Once again, not the right mindset or heartset. You need to keep reminding yourself daily that you are a part of an endless flow of abundance. And as such, you are also contributing to the wellbeing and abundance of others.

Another thing we would like to add is: it may be a good idea to audit the products and services you are currently paying for. If a given product or service doesn't feel right for you, change it. Why pay for something and then experience negative feelings of resentment? Once again, you choose.

This chapter offers a simple lifestyle change rooted in daily mental, emotional, spiritual, and physical practice. You pay for something every day, anyway, right? So, why not be grateful for it? Why not bless all the people who provide you with essential products and services that make your life easier and better and contribute to your wellbeing?

Why not be a happy giver?

And why not use these daily situations to practice an abundance mindset?

You can also support your practice with these simple yet very effective affirmations:

I am in a flow of unlimited abundance.

I love giving and receiving.

I am grateful for the convenient and stress-free life that the services I purchase provide me with.

Thank You Thank You Thank You

There's always more and more money available for me.

I always make good financial decisions.

I always attract the best deals, discounts, products, and services.

I always attract unexpected money.

Money always finds me!

The above affirmations can be used both for spending and receiving money.

It's all about releasing guilt, shame, and any negative inner states around money.

The most practical way to do so is to monitor your inner state as you go about your day. Simply be mindful!

Also, think about it. You will be setting an excellent example for others. So many people feel stressed because of money and take that stress out on other people. Elena is not particularly proud to admit that she, too, experienced many negative states because of money, and it reverberated on her health, wellbeing, and relationships with others.

Then, she blamed money itself and went to another extreme such as money is bad and not spiritual.

In reality, money is neither good nor bad. It's neutral. It just is. It's used to exchange products and services. It's like a messenger of a flow of infinite abundance.

Yes, we agree that money can become bad energy if handed to bad people with unethical intentions.

But, it can also be used to circulate between ethical products and service providers and their customers. It can bring comfort and joy to many people. It all comes down to the people who handle money.

Good people with good intentions definitely don't need to worry about: "Money is bad and not spiritual." Understand that money is just a tool created to support you. And it's one of the expressions and manifestations of your inner abundance and peace.

Cultivate peaceful and neutral inner states. Keep letting go of any negative fear-based and guilt-based mindsets around money, and your life will be forever transformed.

Oh, and as they say: it's not only about money. Abundance also manifests as joy, peace of mind, an abundance of creativity, energy, and innovative solutions.

It also manifests as great relationships filled with love and happy moments.

In other words, your desires are abundance!

Message #4 Don't Help Others without Protecting Your Energy (Important Message for Empaths)

The message we have to share in this chapter may be a bit outside the box for some people. But it may also offer a huge relief and soothe their inner states.

So, before we get into it, we want to make something very clear- yes, we believe in helping others. The genuine desire to help others, backed up by aligned action and good intentions, raises vibrations of everyone involved.

But, since we know that this message will be read by many heart-based, empathetic people, we prefer to dive deeper and share why it's essential to approach helping others from the right mindset and heartset.

Here's what we think is worth discussing and can help many of Elena's beautiful readers who are on the same journey as she is:

-When are you in a position to help others? Should you neglect your own needs to help others?

-Is it right to help others as a business venture and charge for it?

-Should you help others out of obligation alone?

-How to protect yourself from the manipulative energies of other people?

-How to make sure you're doing the right thing and helping someone who can benefit from it?

-Can you help someone without doing anything?

-Can you help someone just by being you?

-Is it OK to brag about how you help other people and how many people you helped?

-Should you help others just for the sake of doing so?

Let's start with the most important one...

-When are you in a position to help others? Should you neglect your own needs to help others?

The short answer is that the first person you need to help is you. It's as simple as that. While many may rebel and say that it's not very spiritual, let us say this- if you really want to help others, you need to be able to do so.

So, the first person you need to help is you. If you want to use money to help others by supporting your favorite charities, you need to have enough to take care of your own needs and the needs of others. Even if you're not a materialistic person, you still need to have enough money to buy food and have a place to stay, right?

And to be able to help people on a bigger scale, using money as a tool, you would first need to take care of your own financial wellbeing and the financial wellbeing of your company or charity you want to start or support.

Of course, money is just one of the tools you can use to help others. It's very powerful and can be used to quickly help those in need of food, shelter, or medical care. There's no doubt about that. It can also be used to pay for someone's education and help them towards a better financial future for themselves and their families.

But our main intention is to open your eyes to how many vehicles there are to help others. There are infinite ways to help yourself and others.

It's all about choosing the vehicle that feels right to you.

For example, some people like to use their time to help others by offering voluntary work for a charity or other organization they support. Some like giving money or food to homeless people. Some may not be able to give much financially, but offer emotional and mental support to help those in need shift their thinking and embrace hope.

Many will say that to help others on a bigger scale, the only thing needed is a lot of money. And yes, as we already said: to help others at the most fundamental level, to help others improve their living conditions, money can work very fast.

But, as judgmental as it may sound...Some people may be given financial help and improve their lives only to manifest themselves back to their old situation of not having anything.

Why? Well, because they haven't changed their habits, mindsets, and energetic principles by which they operate. They haven't changed their awareness.

Hence the importance of helping others spiritually and mentally by assisting them in shifting their awareness. And this is what we believe the world really needs! If you are reading books about the Law of Attraction, mindset, spirituality, and self-development, you are already in the minority of people with a higher level of awareness.

Of course, we don't say you should feel superior because of that and judge those who don't read similar materials.

But, when you think about it, you have something that can raise the planet's vibration. You have all the information you need to transform yourself, embody your desires, become the best version of yourself and help others by sharing your knowledge.

It's really up to you how you decide to approach it. Some people like organizing workshops for their community. Some enjoy sharing their knowledge via books, videos, or social media channels. Technology is changing the world and can be used to help a lot of people, even while you sleep. For example, you could make a video about a spirituality topic you have been learning about, or you could make a motivational or inspirational video and share it with the rest of the world.

Then, the content you create can share your message for you and keep inspiring other people, even while you're doing something else.

That's the wonder (and power) of technology!

And sharing your knowledge and unique story can give someone hope, shift them or even completely transform their lives. Then, they become a better version of themselves and treat themselves and others better. Their transformation has a compound effect.

This is very powerful and can shift awareness and raise the collective vibration!

Conclusion? There's no right or wrong. There are many ways you can help others if you feel called to do so! Simply find a way that feels good to you. Everyone has something they can offer so that the rest of the world can benefit from it.

However, whatever channel you choose, first help yourself. If you're not in a position to help others, focus all, or at least most of your attention on helping yourself.

-Is it right to help others as a business venture and charge for it?

The short answer is, yes, of course, it is!

And if you have a desire to be a heart-centered entrepreneur and build a company or business that helps others, just go for it! Release any shame or guilt around charging for your services.

Does your hairdresser feel guilty about charging you for doing your hair? What about your handyman, mechanic, or any service provider you hire?

Yet, there's still a lot of judgment around charging for spiritual services or heart-based work.

Of course, we are not telling you what to do. We simply intend to open your mind and heart so that you can receive your answers. It's all about following your heart and doing what's right for you.

We've already talked about money and abundance in the last chapter. We briefly mentioned how money in itself is neutral and when handed to and circulating between good, heart-centered people, it can only do good things in the world.

In alignment with that, think about how our world can change and how much good can be created through more and more heart-based businesses? Enterprises that do ethical business pay well their employees and offer great products and services that change people's lives. Those businesses can only do good and make everyone happy.

So, if it's in your heart, if that's what you want to do and feel called to do, give yourself the permission to start by releasing any guilt around charging for your products or services.

It all comes down to asking yourself what you truly desire and releasing any blocks around your desire by taking positive and aligned action. Remember that nobody has the right to judge you, and it's safe to be yourself and follow your desires!

But as always, it's all about choices and putting your wellbeing first. Remember what we said at the beginning of this chapter? You can't help others unless you help yourself first. At the same time, it's not about following some trends. As we are sharing this message, we are aware that many people are being influenced by social media and what others do. Many people choose to become entrepreneurs or start coaching businesses because they think that's what they should or have to do. But they are not passionate about what they do.

Please, own your mind and heart first! We have already told you multiple times that helping others should feel good, and there is an unlimited number of vehicles to do so. So, if you're stuck in a business you're not passionate about, or it's not going well, and you just feel like doing something else, give yourself permission to do so. Choose yourself first. Helping others doesn't have to be about becoming a martyr or suffering. It should be a natural expression of who you are.

And it doesn't have to be about doing something extraordinary. It doesn't have to be about becoming a celebrity entrepreneur or a famous coach if that's not your calling.

You can do extraordinary things via ordinary tasks or jobs. There are many ordinary people nobody knows about, they are not famous, and nobody follows them with a camera, filming their good deeds, but they do lots of good. Why? Because they approach whatever job or task they do with good energy.

The conclusion? You can help others with any job, profession, or business you do. For any task you perform, simply think about the people on the other side and how your work will benefit them.

It's all about your energy. You can be a healer, coach, accountant, fireman, charity worker, chef, waiter, cleaner, CEO, or teacher. Whatever you do, intend to do it well and center your energy. Bless everyone around you. You can use your regular job or any activity (it can also be a hobby) to spread positive vibes and help others.

Some people feel better and more secure by holding a day job that covers their financial needs so that in their free time, they can pursue their ambitions or some kind of activities that help others. Yet, some people prefer to channel all their time and energy into creating a business that supports them, their employees, and their families and, at the same time, offers transformational products or services.

Keep asking yourself what is suitable for you and your life. Remember that you can manifest anything you want, as long as your goal is truly yours, not someone else's.

Elena always recommends you give yourself some quiet reflection and meditation time to tune into your authentic desires and your personalized vehicle to achieve them. There's no right or wrong.

Don't pressure yourself into quitting your day job because some online mentors tell you it's the only way to abundance, success, and happiness. But at the same time, if you're indeed called to build your own business, don't feel bad about charging for your services and going full time with your passion.

Different strokes for different folks. Own your strokes and your authentic self.

The main point of this book is unlimited empowerment. There are infinite ways to live your life while fulfilling your life's mission and helping others just by being you and doing what you do the best you can, from your highest vibration.

-Should you help others out of obligation alone?

Very few people realize this simple spiritual law. The more you force yourself to do something you don't want to do, the more unwanted manifestations you create.

Of course, we don't want to make you feel guilty about your past decisions. And we truly understand that people always do the best they can with what they have available. At the same time, society's pressure and norms and things we should do to stick to certain stereotypes can get us off track.

The number one thing to remember is- help others if you want to. But remember that you need to take care of your own needs first. Also, helping others is not some kind of a contest or a competition. And it doesn't have to be about being a martyr.

-How to protect yourself from the manipulative energies of other people?

The first thing you need to do is keep auditing your thoughts and feelings. In other words, you need to be a master of your awareness. Your awareness will set you free.

There are different levels of awareness and making sure you operate from the highest one will set you on the right track, no matter what you do and where you are.

Whatever vehicle you choose to help others, remember to act from this intention: if you genuinely want to help someone, you want to make sure you do it to help them help themselves. That's the highest level of help you can offer no matter what you do. And you help someone grow and be independent.

Intend to operate from this level of awareness as much as possible, and you'll be genuinely amazed by how your reality transforms!

-How to make sure you're doing the right thing and helping someone who can benefit from it?

So, first things first. How to know you're doing the right thing? You need to know yourself, your values, and what you stand for. You need to have your life philosophy and stick to it. You need to embody what you believe in.

When you know who you are and are grounded in your truth, you attract people who know who they are and what they want.

And you attract people who really appreciate you and whatever you do to help them.

-Can you help someone without doing anything new or extraordinary?

Yes, that is also possible. After all, it doesn't matter what you do, but how you do it. You can help someone just by being you.

Inspiring and motivating others is also a form of help. And you can inspire and encourage someone just by being you. You can embody your truth and do what you were called to do the best you can.

If you don't know what your calling is, for now, don't worry about it. Simply set an intention to find it. For now, give yourself the luxury to mindfully explore different options, learn new things and practice spirituality by doing ordinary tasks or working a regular job in an extraordinary way.

Message #5 Your Desires Are Divine – Time to Release Fear, Guilt, and Shame!

So many people have a burning desire to manifest something, yet they hold themselves back and never even attempt to manifest anything. They block themselves right after they realize or state their desire.

The reason? Well, they feel guilty. Or even ashamed of their desires.

It's like wanting something but feeling bad about it simultaneously. How can you generate positive feelings and positive, aligned actions to manifest something if you keep beating yourself up about it?

As your manifestation angels, we are here to inspire and empower you. Release any feelings of shame or guilt around your desires. Understand that your desires were placed in your heart for a reason! They are yours to have. They are your inner GPS. Your desires are meant to guide you on your journey. When we say "journey," we're not referring merely to your manifestation journey or the moment you reach your goals and manifest your desires.

We are referring to the journey of You. The journey of unleashing your true potential to become the best version of yourself.

For example, Elena had a burning desire to write. And trust us when we say this - it was pretty hard to communicate with her. So many times, we tried to remind her of her genuine desire and goal, and she simply wouldn't listen! Instead, she kept chasing some weird business opportunities far from her true calling and passions.

It took us several years of pretty hard work to make her understand and feel her true calling. We had to guide her to trust herself. Because she didn't feel worthy of following her dreams. She felt like she needed to do something to become worthy of following her writing desire.

But, when you think about it, whatever you want to do, the best time is now, today. Today is the day for you to get started.

If you want to teach your expertise or share your passion with other people, stop worrying and projecting your fears and negative what-ifs.

Instead, ask yourself this question: *If I start today, if I really follow my calling and do what I love, and if I start today, how will my life change one year from now? What about five years from now? Or ten years from now?*

Most people think that it has to be all or nothing, and instead of focusing on what they desire to manifest, they focus on excuses.

"Maybe this is not for me?".

Your logical mind may try to talk you out of following your heart's desires.

Or you may get too caught up in never-ending research and instead of following your heart and your desire, start following other people's opinions.

Wouldn't it be better to use all that time spent on negative worry and negativity to follow your passion and do what you love?

Yes, we understand your earthly obligations. We said that it doesn't have to be all or nothing from day one.

All you need to do is allow yourself to get started and keep placing one foot in front of the other. Keep going.

For example, many creative and spiritual people desire to write, paint, create art, or express themselves via different social media channels. And many people earn a great living doing what they love. So, it's possible!

But of course, we understand that Rome wasn't built in a day. In the dimension we are in as of now, things manifest instantly. But on Earth, things take time to materialize.

But what if it was always easy for you? What if you could manifest your desires instantly, like in our dimension?

Well, your mind wouldn't be able to comprehend it. And you would lose the drive and motivation to pursue new goals and manifest new things. Most of the time, you wouldn't be happy. So, all we can tell you is this- things are arranged the way they are for a reason. It's all for your good!

But to empower you and help you take inspired action, please know that things can move very fast when you fully align yourself and embody your desire. Please re-read the chapter on the embodiment. Use your desire and passion to activate the energy of intention by getting started and promising yourself to be true to yourself.

Now, we can sense some of your fears, especially when it comes to following your passion professionally.

We understand that you may be thinking:

-*"But how will I earn a living, I have a family to support?"*

-*"What if it doesn't work out?"*

-*"What if nobody likes what I do and I make a fool of myself?"*

Well, the solution is very simple. And it's not about risking your finances or your family's wellbeing. It's about taking consistent, aligned action on your desire and thinking about it as a GPS that will take you somewhere amazing. A place that you may not even be able to comprehend yet.

For example, if your desire is to express yourself through writing, videos, blogs, or social media, or perhaps you would like to become a coach or a YouTuber, ask yourself this question:

Can I put in at least half an hour every day?

We're sure you can!

And you can still keep your day job or whatever obligations you have.

Don't make any projections. Simply act on your desire. If it's in your heart, it was placed there on purpose. And it doesn't have to be your final destination. It can be the next step that takes you somewhere else.

Have trust in your angels and the Universe.

Perhaps, your new desire is a sign to start taking aligned action so that you can build up your character and discipline? Maybe it's a sign that will lead you to learn something new?

Never disregard those intuitive downloads and your heart's desires.

And trust us, we are very patient and understanding, explaining all this to you. Elena was difficult. Very stubborn. You can't even imagine the amounts of energy we had to put in to make her embody her desire and take consistent, aligned action.

Although truth to be told, we also needed her as a channel to share our message to help raise the planet's vibration. Because that's the business we're in, after all! And we had to do our part because that's what we wanted to do, that's what we were called to do, and ultimately...we did!

Boy, was it challenging to keep sending all those signals and intuitive downloads to Elena for so many years! Even when we felt ignored for so long, we kept going.

Because we believed. We believed in ourselves, our mission, and our little stubborn Elena! And we knew we had to keep showing up daily while placing one foot in front of the other.

Tune in to the voice of your heart. It will help you release the fears of your mind. Remember that you are safe, loved, and protected. You can still be you and go about your day as you normally do. You can still attend your regular business or day job. And you can still keep moving forward with your desires.

The Universe loves speed, confidence, and conviction.

So, ask yourself: "What can I do today to move forward?"

Now that you see your desire as a GPS, something pure and angelic, meant to guide you, are you willing to follow through?

Activate your desire with intention.

The word intention consists of " in + tension." Because when you first get started on something, you may feel a bit of tension. But all that tension is coming from your mind, and you have the power to release it quickly. Stay focused on your inner GPS and calmly place one foot in front of the other.

Trust yourself and the Universe. Your heart always knows. And trust us when we say this: your angels may feel a bit tired after so many futile attempts to communicate with you and charge your inner GPS with your true desires.

The time is now. Let's go!

In the next chapter, we will share all you need to know about taking action. We feel like many people in the manifesting and LOA community really need it because there are so many misconceptions about taking action.

Message #6 The Science of Taking Aligned Action

It's time to talk about taking action. In the LOA and manifesting community, many people get confused about it, and we're not surprised. Because the information people get comes straight from the spiritual realm and is designed solely for the spiritual realm but is not correctly interpreted and explained for those living in the physical dimension. And so, many souls get lost. They just get stuck in the energy of waiting for their manifestations, get impatient and lose their faith. We don't want this to happen to you.

So, here's how it works:

In the spiritual realm, where all spiritual teachings originate, things can materialize instantly. However, in the physical realm, things can take time. At the same time, the way things work on Earth is to protect people from the tricks their minds can play on them.

Imagine that you could think about something, for example, a million-dollar suitcase lying on your kitchen table. And you could materialize it instantly, just because you were thinking about it.

At the same time, you could think about something negative, such as some weird monsters entering your home, and manifest that vision. Instantly!

Yes, we understand that the above example may seem childish to many people. And it's pretty common sense. But to be honest, the way people on Earth try to practice manifestation sometimes seems childish to us, too (we don't mean to offend anybody, just sharing something that will help you manifest your desires with joy and ease!).

Each dimension has its own set of rules to stick to. Spiritual laws are always the same, but how they operate on the physical plane is slightly different. If you're reading this now, you're both spiritual and physical. And you will get the best results with manifesting by using your "local" earthly laws. Bridge your earthly desires with quantum powers! Combine practical with spiritual, and you will achieve a lot in your life.

Trust us when we say this- you will achieve great things without burning yourself out. You will also spare yourself many negative feelings such as doubt, resentment, and disappointment.

You've probably heard about: ask – believe – receive, right?

We already told you what it means to believe, so let's just quickly re-cap: to believe means to be and live.

So, we can also say: *ask, embody, and receive.*

You embody something by fusing yourself with it. You use all your potential- your thoughts, feelings, and actions.

For example, Elena is on a journey to becoming a successful blogger. We already told you how hard it was for us to empower her to get started on her journey of writing and sharing. But we knew we could use her as our little channel every now and then. To be fair, not everything she writes comes directly from us, and we give her a lot of credit for her ability to learn, research and practice many self-help and spirituality concepts to help her readers.

In the past, Elena would go from one extreme to another. For example, she tried to manifest success without doing anything. She would get way too caught up in spiritual rituals and healing work. There is nothing wrong with spiritual rituals and healing work; we definitely recommend that you stick to whatever works for you.

The problem? She got too caught up in the spiritual and esoteric and lost her ability to stay grounded, make quick and effective decisions, and take actions to move forward.

She even thought she could work for free and give everything away and ended up in a not-so-nice financial situation.

But, she also experienced another extreme. She got into this online entrepreneur thing and got caught up in too much hustle. She wanted to make up for being too woo-woo and focused entirely on taking physical action without any alignment. So, she burned herself out and wasn't very happy.

During that time, she experienced lots of suffering; even though she could manifest financial success, it would never last, and she experienced a lot of fear that her savings and hard work would be taken from her.

Luckily, she woke up just in time and decided to listen to her manifestation angels! One day, she thought: *wait a minute, the word "attraction" contains the word "action"*.

And after studying people who achieved holistic success with LOA and manifesting both well-known LOA gurus, for example, Bob Proctor or Rhonda Byrne, and everyday people who live extraordinary lives thanks to LOA, she finally understood: *you need balance*. You need inner and energy work to understand who you really are, stay connected to the Source, and feel guided all the time. You also need firm and consistent physical activity to stay grounded and keep moving forward.

There's no specific rule for creating balance between action and attraction. We encourage you to practice and figure it all out for yourself.

But, in most cases, you will definitely need both.

Now, to be clear, we say: in most cases.

Because it is definitely possible to manifest out of thin air, and these things happen. Some manifestations may not require any action. We encourage you to believe in magic. But once again, to believe, means to be and live. So, be magic and live magic. Do your part. Do your thing.

However, when it comes to manifesting success, creativity, or financial stability (as well as health and fitness), we recommend you support your spiritual and energy practice with the firm, aligned actions that feel good to you and come from your core.

So, several months ago, we decided to motivate Elena to start a blog. At first, she experienced a lot of resistance because she had negative past experiences with creating websites. Her entrepreneur friends would tell her that blogging was a total waste of time.

By using the Law of Attraction, she could change her thoughts. She'd project herself five years into the future, running a successful blog. She'd visualized emails from happy readers.

She took action from that positive place. And setting up the blog and creating the first posts went very smoothly. Even though she isn't a technical person. There was no stress. She enjoyed every moment of what most of her friends would label as "hard work."

Now, she keeps taking aligned action every day. Even if it's creating a draft for a blog post. That's her rule! Even if life gets busy, she still stays committed to her blog. 15 minutes a day is better than nothing!

Why? Well, because she believes in the compound effect.

You create visible results by taking little steps every day.

Elena uses the same principle for her self-development and spiritual practice. She loves daily meditation and tapping. Even if life gets busy, she will do it because it feels good. And, as always, five minutes a day is better than nothing.

And, in the spiritual realm, there's no such thing as time and linear time anyway. All that matters here is that you stay aligned with your vision daily by taking little baby steps in the direction of your goal.

You calmly place one foot in front of the other.

There's no need to hustle, grind or burn yourself out.

In fact, you could be working fewer hours, but make the hours you work more focused, calm, and productive.

Because the energy from which you take action matters.

We would also like to remind you that there are different strokes for different folks. We are not saying you should copy Elena.

She asked for her path, got her answers, embodied them, and worked behind the scenes because she had faith.

Just like the Universe works behind the scenes to support you (and so do your beautiful Manifestation Angels), you too can do your part by following your mission, rolling up your sleeves, and embracing the power of sexy, behind-the-scenes, consistent work! All from the energy of abundance, peace, and confidence.

Of course, we understand that some days may be a bit challenging. Elena was shocked when her blog went down because of some technical issues. But she quickly grounded and centered herself. She visualized her website working as usual, then called her hosting company and enjoyed her issue being resolved at lightning speed.

We recommend studying the Law of Attraction and different techniques such as affirmations, scripting, and visualizations. Elena did an excellent job on writing numerous books to guide you step by step.

But remember that everyone is different. Some people love to affirm, some love to script, and some love to visualize. Some love to create their own unique manifesting mix.

Give yourself some time and space to learn and experiment. But once you've found something that works for you and something you were called to do, just go for it. Do it every day.

You will experience different periods in your life. For some periods, you will need to focus more on learning. But some, you will need to have a little break from learning new information and tune into your inner GPS and start building and creating your dreams based on what you already know.

You will know when that moment comes. There will be no doubts, and you will be called to take action. You may even experience a massive transformation or instant vibrational shift to change your lifestyle.

But release any feelings of stress and impatience. If your purpose is simply to learn, grow, and experience new techniques at this stage of your life, go for it. Don't beat yourself up like so many people do, simply because they feel bad about not knowing their purpose.

For Elena, it took many years. But even when she didn't know her purpose, she couldn't explain it. She knew and trusted it was already within her. As she stopped worrying about it and focused on taking actions that felt good to her, things moved very fast.

Keep asking yourself this question: "How can I combine the action with attraction?"

"Are there any physical actions I can take every day, even if it's only five minutes a day, to help me feel good, align myself with my goals and move forward?"

"What can I do to embody my desires, starting today?"

"Are there any messages and intuitive downloads I may be receiving that I normally ignore or reject?"

"How would it feel to tune in within me for answers?"

"Do I keep beating myself up for not knowing my purpose?"

"What if my purpose, for now, is to learn more about myself? What if the journey could be my destination?"

"Can I use any LOA techniques to empower my daily actions and thoughts?"

"How can I take action from a higher vibration?"

"Can I replace doubt with belief?"

We hope this chapter helped and inspired you.

Now, it's time to give you even more inner freedom.

If you have ever worried about negative thoughts, the next chapter will give you the relief you deserve!

Message #7 Freedom from Negative Thoughts

This chapter will give you a massive vibration shift. It's time to change your relationship with negative thoughts. Once and for all.

It's time to love yourself, be good to yourself, and stop beating yourself up for having negative thoughts.

So many people in the LOA and manifestation community have this fear: "I'm into positivity and the Law of Attraction. My thoughts become my reality. OMG, I have negative thoughts, so I fear they will manifest. I feel bad. After studying all those positive materials, I still think negative thoughts. I can't move forward. Now, my biggest fear is fearing my fears and negative thoughts".

It's time to say enough! First of all, even the most positive people experience negative thoughts. And the mere fact that you have a negative thought doesn't mean that they will manifest instantly.

Remember what we said in the previous chapter? Imagine you have thought about having a suitcase with million dollars lying on your kitchen table. And it manifests instantly. At the same time, you have thoughts about a burglar robbing your house, and boom! He's right there at your door, robbing you!

Luckily, things don't work that way...

Of course, we're not giving you the green light to think negative thoughts. Be mindful and keep auditing your thoughts. But, understand that they have no power over you, and it's not that they will automatically manifest into something horrible.

Please promise yourself not to feel bad about having negative thoughts. Negative thoughts alone are already harmful to your overall wellbeing. They make you live in fear and keep you stuck. Most people are unaware of spiritual and mind laws, and so, when they have any opposing thoughts, they just stay in them. Their negative thoughts become the GPS that may lead them to places they don't want to go. We're talking unwanted manifestations.

Luckily, negative thoughts don't manifest instantly. So that you can give yourself some time and place to shift to positivity.

Also, be grateful because some negative thoughts appear in your mind to protect you. And some negative thoughts may be beneficial. For example, you may experience negative thoughts about your flight or holiday getting canceled. So, you may choose to protect yourself by getting adequate travel insurance.

This is an example of healthy negative thoughts that lead to specific preventive actions. Personally, we believe in combining practical with metaphysical. So, a person who has negative thoughts about their upcoming travel may choose to change their itinerary, airline, or get the insurance that will give them more peace of mind. At the same time, they may decide to affirm: *"I am safe, I am guided, I am protected, God, angels, and the Universe take care of me."*

The golden rule is- to *take care without worrying.*

But don't choose to dwell on negativity. You are an infinite being, and you have the power to shift your thoughts. Ask yourself: "Can I allow myself to think about the things I love?" or: "Is there something positive I can allow myself to look forward to?".

Keep affirming:

"In this moment, I am safe and protected".

Because it's true. Negativity is often created in your mind because you allow it to travel too much to the past and the future. It's like time traveling that doesn't do any good to you. It's time to say no!

But don't beat yourself up because we can give you a quick manifestation shortcut that will automatically make your thoughts more peaceful and joyful.

You see, your point of attraction is now, in this moment. All you need to do is to BE. Feel the peace and safety around it. Cherish it. Take a few deep breaths. In and out.

Focus all your attention on your heart. Literally, allow yourself to leave your mind and focus on your heart.

Can you feel all negativity dissolving?

Your heart is your true inner GPS. It's your ultimate awareness. Let it guide you.

Whenever you have a problem that needs solving, instead of trying hard to solve it with your mind as soon as possible, allow yourself to enter your heart for a few minutes. Embrace mindfulness. Remind yourself that you're amplifying your manifesting powers by centering your awareness. This exercise will take your manifesting practice to the next level. It will help you be more peaceful, mindful, creative, and productive.

Of course, we realize that some things may require your immediate attention, and you may not always have the time and space to enter your heart. Some situations may need your quick intervention.

But, the more you embrace the present moment, the less negative situations you will manifest, seriously! And so, eventually, you will be able to enter your heart more and more.

Many people fear this approach because they are too scared of losing control. Elena was like that too.

But please understand that you can still attend to your job and daily obligations as you usually do. Simply remind yourself to take a few short breaks several times a day to center yourself. Your reality will start shifting quickly from this new, peaceful and mindful energy. It will feel like magic.

Please re-read this several times and don't reject it because of its simplicity. For many people, this is their missing manifesting piece! Who knows? It could be the same for you!

Remember:

In this moment, you are safe. You have nothing to worry about. You can trust yourself. The past has no power over you. And the future is being created to suit you and your desires.

You are here to experience joy and so spread this joy with other people. You are free. Your past has no more power over you.

Embody that joy by embracing the power of the present moment. Take this chapter and this exercise seriously. It will change your life. All you need to do is to practice it.

Connect to your heart when you wake up. You can still lie in your bed. Remind yourself that you are safe, loved, and well-taken care of. It's your moment and your reality. Whenever you experience a negative thought, instead of feeling bad about it, say to yourself: "Oh, isn't that interesting? It's a reminder to mindfully shift myself into something more empowering!".

And whenever you experience any negative "what if" scenarios, simply shift them into positive "what if".

For example: "What if I apply for a new job but won't get it?" can become: "What if I apply for a new job and learn something new and discover a new method of doing job interviews?" or" What if I apply for a new job, get accepted and double my salary?".

We hear people complaining: "Oh, I can't visualize, I can't affirm...."

But humans always visualize and affirm. It's just that those unaware of spiritual laws keep affirming and visualizing automatically focusing on the negative.

Well, it's time to shift into something more empowering. Play it as if it was a game. Start going to the spiritual gym. Yes, you will probably miss some days, and some days may be cheat days. Forgive yourself and simply move forward the best you can.

Because the power of the present moment always awaits you. And when you connect to it, all the past negativity is gone. Resolved. Vanished.

And finally, here's a little tip from Elena. She simply keeps affirming: "Only my positive thoughts manifest." Because after discovering what we shared through her with you in this chapter, negativity has no power over you.

And you can take it one step further by affirming and embodying your new truth: *Only my positive thoughts manifest!*

You are infinite. You are powerful. Nothing can stop you. And you have the right to be yourself and fulfill your desires.

Because you exist. Because you are. And because you understand that negative thoughts have no power over you. They are just a signal to help you shift into positivity, but this time, you will reach even higher!

Message #8 The Law of You- It's Time to Create Your Own Manifesting Rules! (Because You Can!)

What is the best method to manifest the life you love? What is the ultimate secret? How can you find the best teacher or mentor for your LOA journey? What books and materials are worth studying? Maybe you should attend some events or hire a manifestation coach.

It's easy to get confused with so many paths you could explore!

Now, most people want the best and the fastest way to reach their goals. Of course, we totally understand you want to manifest your desires as fast as possible. Why wouldn't you? And the good news is that you totally can. The Universe can work at lightning speed for you. That is not a problem. But, be mindful of one thing. Things take more time because the wise Universe knows you need to learn specific lessons that will help you expand. Never stop embodying your truth. Have trust in the process!

When it comes to choosing a teacher, a book, or a course, there's no right or wrong. Follow your heart and decide to learn from people whose energies resonate with yours. It's as simple as that.

Also, be mindful of this spiritual truth- you need to create the Law of You. Yes, you can study different spiritual laws: the Law of Attraction, Assumption, Gratitude, and whatnot, and learn about these laws from different teachers. We admire your passion for learning and growing and definitely encourage you to stick to the path of spiritual growth.

But remember that the best law is the Law of You. Because it's your unique energy that will manifest the life you want! Authors, coaches, and teachers can guide you and give you some steps and frameworks to follow. But it's always up to you how you decide to take your journey.

What you believe in becomes your truth. It becomes the truth for you in your reality.

At the beginning of her journey, Elena felt very confused by so many contradictions in the LOA community. She tried to figure out the right way and wanted to find the right teacher. But she soon realized that they were all right.

They studied the spiritual laws, practiced them, and shared what worked for them. Now, Elena follows the same approach. She writes about and shares the methods and techniques that she tested and found effective. She believes it's a great way to start for her readers. But she always encourages them to create their own way, be their own teachers and mentors and write their own life scripts!

You have the final say. What you learn about you can choose to accept or reject. You need to activate your own inner mentor. That inner voice of your being that wants only the best for you. That always protects you and treats you like a loving parent. Even if things don't go your way, you can soothe your inner state and keep moving forward without feeling disappointed or resentful.

We want you to approach LOA from a new perspective: *live it, test it, embody it*. And focus on what works for you. Learn from other people and be grateful for their knowledge and teachings. But do your part by choosing to be yourself. Embrace the Law of You. Have the courage to create Your Own Rules. Yes, creating your own rules is totally allowed!

For example, recently (we mentioned this in the chapter about negative thoughts), Elena decided that only her positive thoughts manifest. This is what she believes in, and this is what she shares. It IS her truth! It also gave her a fantastic sense of freedom from negative thoughts! She simply decided that negative thoughts have no power over her and only her positive thoughts manifest. She turned it into her law. Now, she is in the early stages of sharing it to inspire others.

What about you? Can you create your own rules? You can decide what manifestation methods and techniques you like or don't like. You can choose the ones that work for you, study them, test them, and take them to the next level. You don't have to know them all intellectually. All you need to do is take small baby steps and keep testing different laws for yourself. Oh, and did we already tell you that you can't fail? There is no such thing as failure. It simply doesn't exist. You succeed, or you learn. That's all there is to it!

Create the Law of You. Write your own manifestation protocols right now. As long as you are not hurting others and are following your true desires, you are good to go!

So, what would it feel like to be your own mentor and coach? What about having your own manifestation system?

Finally, let us give you freedom from one more manifesting block: "What will others think of me?"

Release it right here, right now. Other people's thoughts create their reality. But right now, if we're not mistaken, we are talking about your reality, right?

And you create your reality with your thoughts, not someone else's thoughts, correct?

So, be yourself. Embrace the Law of You. Give yourself the luxury of being yourself. You write the script of your life, and we are always here to guide you.

It's safe to be YOU.

It's safe to honor your PATH.

It's safe to shine your light!

Nobody has the right to judge you, and you have the right to be yourself!

Until next time we meet, hopefully in one of Elena's new books!

Stay happy, healthy, abundant, and strong,

We love you, we pray for you, and we want only the best for you,

Love and Light

Elena & Manifestation Angels

Conclusion – Trust Yourself

Keep expanding and keep moving forward!

Watch your energy transform.

Embody your desires.

Be your desires.

Affirm your desires with what you do and how you think about yourself, as well as the energy you spread, not only with what you say.

Don't get discouraged or impatient if it takes longer to manifest your desires; the journey itself is your destination. It's all about finding your own way of manifesting. As you explore yourself and your manifestation abilities, you become a better person. You are kind to yourself and others while cultivating a positive mindset infused with endless gratitude. That alone is a gift to those around you!

Keep practicing what you have learned. Keep sharing these concepts with others. Together we can change the world by collectively enhancing our planet's vibration.

I genuinely hope that this book inspired you and gave you new tools to expand your consciousness and raise awareness.

You are limitless, you are powerful, and you are amazing!

I believe in you and wish you all the best on your journey. If you have a few minutes, I'd really appreciate it if you could leave me a short review on Amazon. Let other LOA readers in our community know who this book can help, how, and why.

Thank You, Thank You, Thank You,

I hope we "meet" again,

Much love,

Elena

Join Our Manifestation Newsletter and Get a Free eBook

To help you AMPLIFY what you've learned in this book, I'd like to offer you a free copy of my LOA Workbook – a powerful, FREE 5-day program (eBook & audio) designed to help you raise your vibration while eliminating resistance and negativity.

To sign up for free, visit the link below now: www.loaforsuccess.com/newsletter

You'll also get free access to my inspirational LOA Newsletter to help you stay high vibe.

Through this email newsletter, I regularly share all you need to know about the manifestation mindset and energy.

Plus, whenever I release a new book, you can get it at a deeply discounted price.

To sign up for free, visit the link below now:

www.loaforsuccess.com/newsletter

If you happen to have any technical issues with your sign up, please email me at:

support@LOAforSuccess.com

More Books & Workbooks by Elena G. Rivers:

369 Manifesting Guided Journal

Ready to Speed Up Your Manifestations in 33 Days or Less?

Now available on Amazon:

www.ingramcontent.com/pod-product-compliance
Lightning Source LLC
Chambersburg PA
CBHW072103110526
44590CB00018B/3295